WHAT ON EARTH?

BIRDS

Explore, create, and investigate

Mike Unwin

Pau Morgan

QEB

Meet all the different types of birds on page 6.

Contents

What is a Bird?

Bird Food

Find out how different birds fly on page 18.

Make your own flying bird on page 20.

Discover how birds can use their beaks on page 25.

Make a winter birdbath on page 31.

Learn all about eggs on page 40.

Bird Life and Behavior

Enjoying Birds

See the different tracks and clues birds leave behind on page 56.

Read the story of the king of birds on page 58.

Bird Poems

What do you know about birds?
How do they make you feel?

The Eagle

He clasps the crag with crooked hands;

Close to the sun in lonely lands,

Ringed with the azure world, he stands.

The wrinkled sea beneath him crawls;

He watches from his mountain walls,

And like a thunderbolt he falls.

(ALFRED LORD TENNYSON 1809-1892)

There was an Old Man with a Beard

There was an Old Man with a beard,

Who said, "It is just as I feared!

Two Owls and a Hen,
four Larks and a Wren,

Have all built their nests
in my beard".

(EDWARD LEAR 1812–1888)

Can you write a bird poem?

Meet the Birds

The first birds appeared on Earth about 150 million years ago. Their **ancestors** were small dinosaurs called theropods.

These dinosaurs first grew feathers to keep warm. Then, over millions of years, their bodies slowly changed. Their front legs developed into wings, their bones grew lighter, and their feathers grew longer, to help them fly.

Today, there are more than 10,000 types of bird.

Water Birds

Lots of birds can swim. Ducks, swans, cormorants, and many other water birds have special webbed feet to help them paddle through the water.

Flightless Birds

Some birds can't fly. An emu's wings are too small and floppy to flap in the air. But its long legs help it to run very fast.

Birds of Prey

Many birds live by eating other animals.
These include hawks, buzzards, and eagles.
They all have sharp claws and hooked beaks
to catch, kill, and eat their prey.

Scientists generally sort birds into 30 different groups.

Songbirds

Birds can be very good singers. Some, such as larks and
warblers, may not have bright colors to show off with.
Instead, they use their beautiful songs to impress.

Night Birds

A few birds, such as owls and
nightjars, come out only at
night. During the day, they
hide away and snooze. Most
night birds have big eyes for
seeing in the dark. Their
camouflage colors help keep
them safe and undisturbed
during the day.

All Shapes and Sizes

Birds come in many shapes and sizes. Some are taller than you are. Others are small enough to fit in a matchbox. Here are some of the most amazing.

The bee **hummingbird** is the world's smallest bird. It weighs just 1/20th of an ounce (1.4 g)—that's less than two paper clips. It beats its tiny wings so fast that they make a humming noise as it flies.

The **ostrich** is the world's biggest bird. It can stand over 6 1/2 feet (2m) high. One of its huge eggs could make an omelet for 24 people.

The **wandering albatross** has the longest **wingspan** of any bird. Its wings measure more than 10 feet (3 m) from tip to tip—that's about one and a half times as long as your bed. It can glide over the ocean for hours without flapping.

A male **quetzal** has a very long tail. It wiggles like a snake, catching the attention of females as it flies around in the forest.

A **harpy eagle** has feet bigger than your hands and claws longer than a grizzly bear's. It uses them to catch monkeys in the treetops.

A **pelican** has the longest beak of any bird. It uses this to scoop up fish from the water. A sack of skin underneath helps to store its catch—just like a shopping bag.

Stilts get their name for their very long legs. They use them for wading in shallow water without getting their feathers wet.

Parts of a Bird

A bird's body is specially built for flying. Instead of front legs, it has wings, and its skeleton is very light to help keep it in the air.

A bird's beak is very light in weight. It is covered in a lightweight shell and has many air pockets inside it.

Birds have excellent eyesight. Their eyes are large and are fixed firmly in their sockets, so a bird has to turn its head to look around.

A bird has a big breastbone, or sternum, to support the strong muscles needed for flapping its wings.

Birds have big hearts. That's because flying takes extra energy so they need to pump blood quickly around their bodies.

A bird's legs and feet are mostly bare, with claws on their toes to help them grip. When birds fly, they fold their legs up underneath their body.

Most of a bird's body is covered in feathers. Feathers do many jobs— they keep the bird warm, help it to fly, and show off its colors.

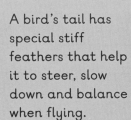

Birds have excellent hearing. Their ears are small openings on the side of their heads, covered in feathers.

A bird's tail has special stiff feathers that help it to steer, slow down and balance when flying.

How to Draw a Bird

Learn to draw a bird using simple shapes.

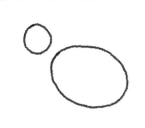

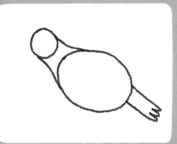

1. Draw two ovals. A big one for the body and a small one for the head.

2. Draw smooth lines to link the head to the body, and add a tail.

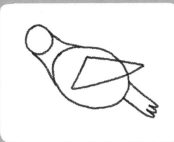

3. Add a triangle shape for the folded wing.

4. Add the beak, the eye, and the legs and feet.

5. Color it in!

Make different birds by using different shapes!

What shapes do you need to make a stork?

Birds Around the World

Birds live in every corner of the world. Some are **adapted** to living in special places, others are found everywhere.

Atlantic puffins are found on steep cliffs around the North Atlantic. One puffin can carry more than ten fish in its colorful beak.

The **bald eagle** is the national bird of the USA. This bird of prey is not really bald, but its snow-white head looks bald from a distance.

The **scarlet macaw** lives in the Amazon rainforest. These forests have more types of bird than anywhere else in the world. In Colombia alone, there are over 1,900 different **species**.

The **roadrunner** lives in the deserts of North America. It is a very fast runner that likes to catch its food on the ground.

Emperor penguins live in the **Antarctic**. Winter temperatures here drop below −58 °F (−50 °C). Brrr! They huddle together to keep from freezing.

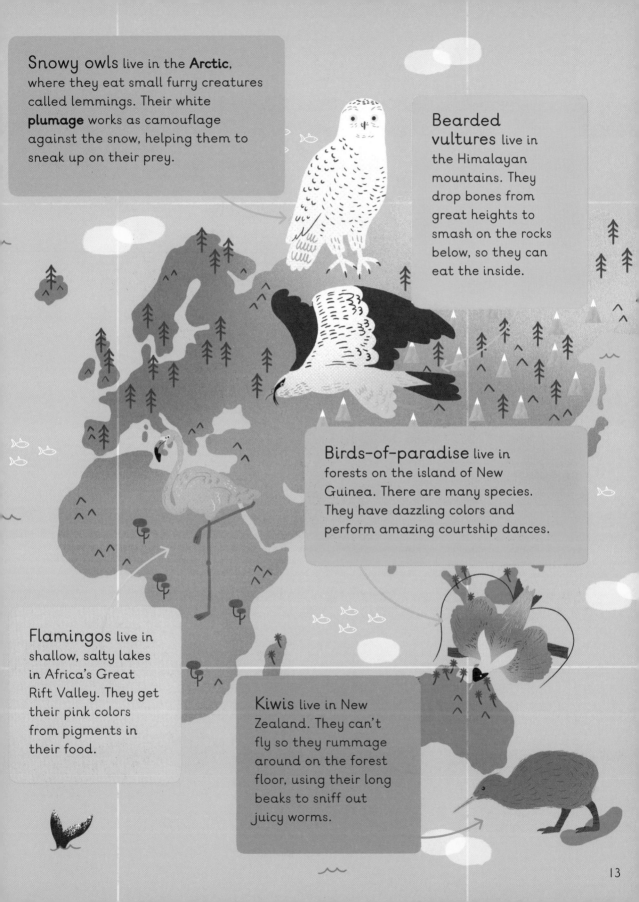

Snowy owls live in the **Arctic**, where they eat small furry creatures called lemmings. Their white **plumage** works as camouflage against the snow, helping them to sneak up on their prey.

Bearded vultures live in the Himalayan mountains. They drop bones from great heights to smash on the rocks below, so they can eat the inside.

Birds-of-paradise live in forests on the island of New Guinea. There are many species. They have dazzling colors and perform amazing courtship dances.

Flamingos live in shallow, salty lakes in Africa's Great Rift Valley. They get their pink colors from pigments in their food.

Kiwis live in New Zealand. They can't fly so they rummage around on the forest floor, using their long beaks to sniff out juicy worms.

Fluffy, Flying Feathers

Other animals can sing, fly, and make nests, but only birds have feathers. There are different types of feathers and together they do many different jobs.

Feathers are very light and can bend without breaking. They are made of a tough, lightweight material called keratin, just like our fingernails.

A bird's plumage helps to protect it. Tiny, fluffy feathers called "down" trap warm air against the skin, while larger ones on top form an outer layer to keep out wind and rain.

Always wash your hands after touching feathers.

An eider duck lines its nest with its soft down feathers to keep its chicks warm. Eiderdown is used to stuff pillows and duvets. It is one of the warmest natural materials on Earth.

The feathers on a bird's wings and tail are big and stiff. These are called flight feathers. When a bird flaps its wings they push against the air to help it take off and fly forward.

Some birds grow twice as many feathers in winter to keep warm.

The long "tail" of a male peacock is not really a tail. It's made of special ornamental feathers called "tail coverts" that lie on top of the real tail underneath. A male peacock spreads out his special feathers in a beautiful fan to attract females.

A bird's feathers as a whole are called its plumage.

Not all feathers are colorful. The potoo is a night bird from South America. By day, its camouflage colors make it look just like a tree stump. This helps it to hide from danger.

Did You Know?

One tundra swan had the most feathers ever counted on any bird: 25,216. Can you imagine counting them?

Feathers in Focus

Feathers are amazing! Find a nice, big feather and take a closer look to discover just what makes it so special.

The **shaft** is the long, stiff middle part of the feather. Its bare end attaches to the bird's skin.

The vane is made up of **barbs**—thin strands that cling together.

The flat parts on either side are called the **vane**.

Every year a bird loses all its feathers then grows a whole new set. This is called **molting**.

Barbules are tiny hooks which make the barbs stick together. You can see them with a magnifying glass.

Try this

Wave a feather back and forth as fast as you can. Do the same thing with a pencil. Which is harder to wave?

What happens?

The feather is harder to wave because the air pushes against its broader surface. This is called **air resistance**: it's what helps birds to take off and fly.

Make a Feathery Owl Mask

Make an owl mask.
Hoot, hoot!

Tool Kit

- white cardstock
- colored paper
- colored pencils
- scissors
- glue stick
- piece of elastic
- tape or staples
- feathers (e.g. from old pillows or craft stores)

What To Do

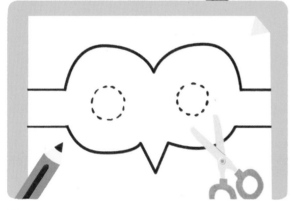

1 Trace the owl head template from page 61 onto a piece of folded cardstock. Cut it out and unfold it.

2 Ask an adult to help cut out eye holes. Then color in feather patterns around them using the template on page 61.

3 Decorate your mask. Cut out and stick down some paper or craft feathers. Stick one big feather in each top corner.

4 Ask an adult to help fix the elastic to the back of the tabs on either side of your mask, using tape or staples.

Up, Up, and Away

How birds fly depends on how they live. Some fly fast, some fly slow. Some fly high, some fly low. Some can do amazing things with their wings.

The **peregrine falcon** is the world's fastest flyer. It folds its wings in a heart shape, and dives through the air at more than 155 miles (250 km/h) to catch other birds in flight. That's faster than a racecar!

Kestrels hover in midair, searching the ground below for mice and **voles**, their favorite food. They fly into a strong breeze and flap their wings lightly to stay in one spot in midair.

Penguins flap their wings under water, using them like **flippers.** They can't fly on land, but below the water their wings help them move very fast.

A **Hummingbird** can beat its wings over 60 times a second. This high-speed flapping lets it hover in midair while it sips nectar from flowers with its long beak.

Vultures have very broad wings. They spread them wide to catch warm air currents, called **thermals**, which rise from the ground. This way they can fly for hours without using up energy by flapping.

Swifts feed on tiny, flying bugs. They only need to touch down when it is time to make their nests and lay eggs. Some spend more than a year in the air without landing at all.

Look how fast they are!

Did You Know?
A vulture in Africa holds the world record for high-flying, at an amazing 36,988 feet (11,274 m). That's higher than **Mount Everest** and higher than most airplanes fly!

Make a Flying Bird

Make a simple bird out of paper and a straw, then have fun trying to make it fly!

Tool Kit

- one paper straw
- paper or cardstock
- scissors
- colored pens or pencils
- tape

What To Do

My bird is going to be a falcon.

1 Trace the wing, head, tail, and **rudder** templates from page 60 onto paper or cardstock and cut out.

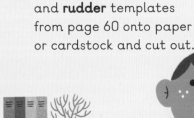

2 Decorate each section to look like a bird. You could draw feathers on the wings and tail, or add eyes and a beak to the head.

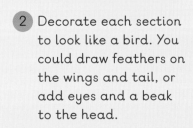

3 Tape the wings across the front third of the paper straw.

4 Next, tape the tail to the back.

5 Place the rudder vertically over the tail and tape in place.

6 Cut a slit in the straw (where shown) then slide the head piece into it.

7 Try launching your bird from somewhere high. How far does it fly?

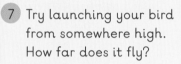

Try This

Can you make any changes to help your bird fly better? You could use different templates to make different birds. For instance, you could give it long wings like a seagull or curved wings like a swift. Or you could give it a longer beak, like a stork. Which ones fly best?

How far can you make your bird fly?

Did You Know?

A magnificent frigatebird is a seabird with very long wings that spends hours flying without flapping. Its body is so light that its feathers weigh more than its skeleton.

Feeling Hungry

All kinds of food are on the menu for birds. Some eat fruit and seeds. Others eat insects, fish, and even other birds.

A sparrow feeds on seeds. Its strong beak can crack open the hard husk to get at the soft, tasty part inside.

A woodpecker feeds on grubs and beetles under tree bark. It climbs tree trunks to dig them out.

An owl feeds on mice. It sleeps all day, then comes out at night to hunt.

A swallow feeds on flying insects and other bugs. It zooms around to catch them in midair.

A hawk feeds on other birds. It chases them through the air and grabs them in its sharp talons.

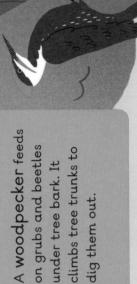

A blue tit feeds on caterpillars. It hangs upside down, searching for them among twigs and leaves.

Did You Know?

Jays eat acorns and they have an amazing memory. During autumn, a jay may bury 5,000 acorns for its winter food supply. Months later, when a jay gets hungry, it can remember where it hid most of them and digs them up again.

A blackbird feeds on worms. It hops around, listening to them moving underground. When it hears something, it sticks its beak into the soil to grab it.

A mallard is a duck that feeds on tiny **minibeasts** and plant seeds found in shallow water. It scoops them up in its beak.

A heron eats fish and frogs. It waits patiently in, or near, the water then lunges out with its long neck and sharp beak, ambushing them.

Fitting the Bill

A bird's beak is a special tool for feeding and finding food. Just by looking at a bird's beak you can often figure out what it eats.

A bird's beak can also be called a bill.

A **curlew** feeds on worms along the seashore. It uses its long beak to feel deep into the mud. The tip of the beak is sensitive, so it can detect and grab hidden, wriggling worms.

A **shoebill** has a huge beak shaped like a shoe. It lives in swamps in Africa and uses its beak to scoop up fish, frogs, and even baby crocodiles from the swampy water.

A **kingfisher** has a long, sharp beak shaped like a dagger. It uses this to spear fish when it dives into the water.

A **toucan's** huge beak allows it to reach out for fruit in all directions without moving from its branch.

Tools of the Trade

Some birds' beaks work just like the tools that you have around your home. Can you match each bird with its tool? Answers on page 63.

Beaks

1. A flamingo has a special mesh inside its bill to filter tiny food from water.

2. A parrot has a strong bill that can break into the hardest fruit.

3. A shoveler has a flat bill which scoops up tiny creatures from the water's surface.

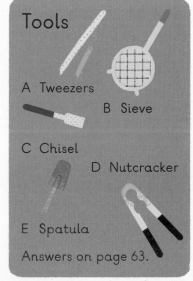

Tools

A Tweezers

B Sieve

C Chisel

D Nutcracker

E Spatula

Answers on page 63.

4. A woodpecker has a stout bill to push under tree bark and find insects hiding there.

5. A warbler has a fine, delicate bill to reach between leaves and pick out little insects.

Make a Pop-up Puffin Card

The puffin is called the "clown of the sea" because of its funny beak. Make your own puffin with a beak that opens and closes.

What To Do

1 Fold a white piece of cardstock in half.

2 Cut a 2-inch (5 cm) slit along the middle of the folded edge, using scissors.

3 Fold back the two triangular flaps on either side of the cut.

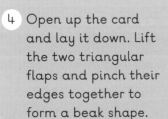

4 Open up the card and lay it down. Lift the two triangular flaps and pinch their edges together to form a beak shape.

Make the beak stick up.

 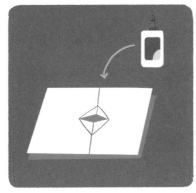 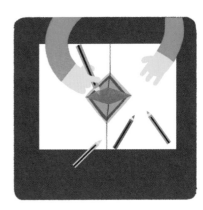

5 Close the card and fold the two triangular flaps neatly inside. Now open it up again. You should have a beak that opens and closes when you open and close the card.

6 Glue a piece of pink cardstock behind the white one. You can see the pink through the open beak. This is the inside of your puffin's mouth.

7 Use pencils or pens to color in the puffin's beak, as shown.

Now send your card to a fellow bird lover, or keep it for yourself.

8 Draw the shape of a puffin around the beak. Use a black marker to color in the black parts. Don't forget the bright orange feet!

Did You Know?
- A puffin can hold 12 tiny fish in its beak at once.
- A baby puffin is called a puffling.
- A puffin can dive down 200 feet (60 m) to catch fish underwater. That's more than the length of an Olympic swimming pool.

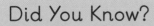

27

A Garden Feast

Birds will visit your school or yard if you offer them food to eat. This is helpful in winter, when wild food is harder to find.

Seeds

Mixed birdseed is full of energy for birds. You can scatter it on a bird table, or fill up a bird feeder or window tray.

Sugary Treats

If you live in North America, hummingbirds might visit your garden. These tiny birds love to sip nectar from flowers. You can put up special feeders to give them sweet sugar water, just like nectar.

Fallen Fruit

In winter, leave out old apples and other fallen fruit on the ground. Blackbirds and starlings use their strong beaks to peck out tasty chunks.

Where to Eat

Some small birds, such as tits, chickadees, and goldfinches, like to feed from hanging feeders. Other birds, such as pigeons, sparrows, and starlings, prefer to feed on flat surfaces.

Make a Bird Cake

Give birds a winter treat by making them a special cake packed with all their favorite **ingredients**.

What To Do

Tool Kit

- 3 ounces (85 g) fat (suet or lard—leave out to soften first)
- handful of wild birdseed, raisins, bird peanuts, grated cheese
- mixing bowl and wooden spoon
- clean yogurt cup
- string

1 Break up the fat into small pieces. Mix in all the other ingredients using a wooden spoon. Squeeze it with your fingers so that the fat holds it all together.

2 Ask a grown-up to make a small hole in the bottom of a clean yogurt cup. Double the string over, tie a knot at the end, and thread it through the hole so that the knot is on the inside.

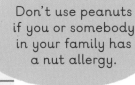

Don't use peanuts if you or somebody in your family has a nut allergy.

4 When it has set solid, hang it somewhere in your yard for the birds to enjoy.

3 Put the mixture into the yogurt cup. Then put into the fridge.

29

Making a Splash

Birds need water to survive. They drink it and use it to keep clean. You can help by putting out clean water in your garden.

A Flying Bath

Birds bathe regularly to keep their feathers in good condition. Some splash around in a pond or puddle, others spread out their wings and feathers to catch a rain shower. Swallows take a bath on the wing, dipping quickly into a pond then flying up again.

Thirsty Birds

Birds drink in different ways. Insect-eating birds get most of the moisture they need from their juicy food. Seed-eaters have a drier diet, so they have to drink more regularly. Most birds drink by taking a sip then lifting their head so it trickles down their throat. Pigeons are different: they immerse their bill in the water and suck it up.

Did You Know?

Sandgrouse nest in the desert where there is no water nearby. They have a clever way to give their chicks a drink. Every evening they fly to a **waterhole** and wade in up to their belly. They return to their nest, where the chicks sip the water from their feathers.

Make a Winter Birdbath

Make a birdbath that will work for birds all winter.

Tool Kit

- three bricks
- snow shovel (if it's been snowing)
- shallow metal dish, bowl, or dustbin lid (with sloping edges)
- large stone
- tea light candle and matches
- warm clothes
- warm water

What To Do

1. Find a place that is flat and sheltered from the wind. Clear away any snow on the ground.

2. Arrange the three bricks into a triangle shape. Ask an adult to place a lit candle in the middle.

3. Rest your dish or bowl on the bricks and fill with warm water—not too deep.

Birdbath Safety

- Keep your birdbath clean to help birds stay healthy. Change the water regularly and wash it out once a week.
- Choose a safe spot for your bird bath. It should be positioned so that birds can look out for danger in all directions. It should also be near cover, such as bushes, where they can fly for protection.

4. Place the stone in the middle to give the birds somewhere to perch.

Bird Babies

When birds breed they make a nest where the female then lays her eggs. When the chicks hatch, their parents look after them until they can take care of themselves.

Pairing Up

Before **breeding**, a male and female bird must first get together. Male birds attract females in different ways. Some dance, some sing, and some, like this lyrebird from Australia, show off their beautiful feathers.

Building Skills

Weaver birds are talented builders. They take long pieces of grass in their beaks and **weave** them carefully together to make a round nest. They arrange straw and feathers for a soft lining and leave a small hole on one side so they can fly in and out.

If a bird's eggs get too cold, they won't hatch.

Cozy Eggs

Some birds lay just one egg. Others, like this quail, may lay 12 or even more. Adult birds keep their eggs warm by sitting on them. This is called **incubation**.

Breaking Out

The baby blue tits in this nest
have just broken out of their eggs.
They are blind and featherless
when they first hatch, but they
can open their beaks wide. They
make a loud cheeping noise to beg
their parents for food.

Did You Know?

A pair of blue tits may
collect more than 1,000
caterpillars every day to
feed their chicks.

CHEEP
CHEEP CHEEP
CHEEP

Leaving Home

A baby bald eagle flaps its wings to
practice flying. When its wings are
strong enough it will fly away from
the nest and start to look after itself.
It is called a fledging.

Nests

Birds use many different kinds of nests.
Many use holes in trees or riverbanks.
A few don't make any nests at all.

Long-tailed tits make their soft round nests from moss, spiders' webs, and feathers. One pair may gather more than 1,500 feathers for their nest.

A **woodpecker** uses its strong beak to dig a hole in the soft wood of an old tree trunk, then it lays its eggs inside.

The **killdeer** lays its eggs in a small hollow that it scrapes in the ground. Its spotted pattern camouflages it as stones, so it can escape the beady eyes of enemies.

Tailorbirds make a nest by stitching two big leaves together. They use their beaks as a needle and a fine piece of grass as thread.

Eared grebes gather weed from the water to build a floating nest. They attach it to a water plant growing on the bottom to stop it from drifting away.

Barn swallows collect mud from puddles in their beaks. They use it to make nests on the wall of a building. The mud dries and hardens, like clay. They add straw and feathers for a soft lining.

Did You Know?

Sociable weavers are small African birds that work together to build one huge nest of grass, up to 13 feet (4 m) across. It's like an apartment block for birds. Inside there are many individual nest chambers—enough for up to 100 pairs.

Helping Birds Build

At the beginning of nesting season, birds collect materials to build their nests. You can help by providing some useful bits and pieces.

dry grass and straw

twigs—stiff ones and bendy ones

bits of bark, moss, and dead leaves

spiderwebs (from a shed or garage)

hair—save some clippings if you have a haircut

yarn or string

feathers (from an old pillow)

mud (in a shallow bowl)

Watch to see which birds choose which materials.

Try This

Leave out your material in easy-to-see places. You could dangle string or hair from branches, or leave twigs and grass in the middle of the yard. Keep checking to see whether anything has been taken.

Make a Bird Nest

Make a bird nest using only what you find outside, just like a bird does.

Tool Kit

- newspaper
- a park or yard
- string
- materials to build a nest
- mud

What To Do

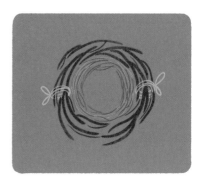

1. Gather things to build a nest. Use bendy twigs, long grass, bark, dead leaves, moss, and pine needles. Lay them all out on newspaper.

2. Loop the bendy twigs into a nest shape. Weave them together or tie them in place using string.

3. Shape some grass or smaller twigs into a smaller loop. Wedge this inside the larger loop. Spread it out to form the base of the nest.

Try different materials to see what works best.

4. Fill out the base with more material. Stick together with mud.

5. Once your nest is done, try to fix it in a tree or bush. Does it stay?

Try This

Use any bits of shiny paper you find to decorate your nest. Magpies do this too.

Make a Bird Home

You can recycle an old carton to make a fun house for a bird.

Tool Kit

- empty milk or juice carton
- stapler
- masking tape
- cloth or rag
- brown shoe polish
- scissors
- glue
- bits of dry moss and bark
- sharpened pencil
- string
- hole punch
- pencil
- helpful grown-up

What To Do

1. Rinse out the carton and let it dry.

2. Close the top of the carton and staple it shut.

3. Cut pieces of masking tape the length of your finger. Stick them all over the carton, letting the edges overlap slightly.

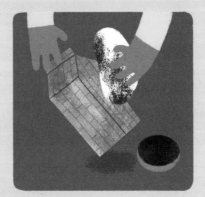

4. Dip the cloth into shoe polish and dab it all over the carton, so it looks like bark. Let the polish dry.

5. Ask a grown-up to help you cut a circle about 1 inch (2.5 cm) in diameter in one side of the carton, about 4 inches (10 cm) above the bottom. This is the entrance hole.

Hang it high so that cats can't reach it.

6 Poke a few holes in the bottom of the carton with a pencil, for drainage, and two in the top, for air.

7 Glue some moss or bark on the outside.

8 Use the hole punch to make a hole in the peak at the top of the carton and thread some string through it. Tie a knot in the string and hang it from a tree.

Try This

Different kinds of birds prefer different size entrances. Wrens, chickadees, tits, and bluebirds like a small hole.

Robins and flycatchers prefer an open front. You can try making several bird homes, each with a different entrance.

Eggs-periments

All birds lay eggs. Inside each one is an **embryo**. It grows bigger and bigger until one day it breaks out as a baby bird.

An egg's hard shell prevents the soft insides from drying out. It has tiny holes, or pores, that let in air so the embryo can breathe.

The albumen, or egg white, provides protection for the embryo and yolk.

The yolk provides food for the embryo.

The embryo is a tiny, growing baby bird.

Hens' eggs

If you crack a hen's egg into a shallow bowl, you can see the albumen (the egg white) and the yolk, but there's no embryo. Hens' eggs that we eat are not **fertilized**, which means there is no baby bird growing inside them.

Eggs are stronger than you think.

Remember, birds must sit on them to keep them warm until they hatch.

Try This

How strong is an eggshell? Wrap an egg in cling film then hold it sideways in the palm of your hand. Close your fist around it and squeeze. Can you break it?

Paint an Egg

Birds' eggs come in many different colors and patterns. Make your own colorful eggs.

Tool Kit

- white eggs x 6
- saucepan
- cups x 6
- food coloring
- vinegar
- tongs
- empty egg carton
- apron (or old clothes)
- newspapers

What To Do

1. Place your eggs in a pan of water on the stove. Ask a grown-up to bring it to a boil then simmer for ten minutes. Remove from heat and add cold water to stop the eggs from cooking.

2. Lay out old newspapers then fill the cups halfway with hot water. Add one teaspoon of vinegar and one of food coloring to each cup.

3. Place one boiled egg in each color for five minutes. Lift it out with the tongs and you have a perfectly dyed egg.

Try This

Draw on your egg with a wax crayon before you dip it. Your drawing will appear in white after the egg is dyed. Or wrap rubber bands around your egg before dipping to create a stripy egg.

Feathered Dancers

Some birds dance to show they are ready for breeding. In some **species** the male dances alone, showing off his colors. In others, the male and female dance together.

Fancy Footwork

Blue-footed boobies walk slowly around each other in circles, lifting up their bright blue feet. They also flap their wings and point their beaks in the air.

Inside Out and Upside Down

Male birds-of-paradise keep their special dancing feathers tucked away. When it's time to perform, they fan these feathers out, revealing surprising shapes and hidden colors.

Leaping Cranes

Japanese cranes jump up in the air together, flapping their wings. Then they take turns pointing their beaks down at the ground and up at the sky.

Dance Like a Bird

Invent your own special bird dance by yourself or with a friend. Remember: birds don't worry about looking silly, so neither should you!

Dance Rules

Most bird dances have rules. Follow these rules when you make your dance.

- You can use props (e.g: flowers, sticks, wooden spoons), but you can't pick up or hold anything using your hands.

- You can make any noises you like—except for words.
- Try not to touch your partner. If you bump into each other you have to start again.

Look the Part

Birds have all sorts of special tricks to help them stand out when dancing, such as hidden colorful feathers and big, stomping feet! Dress up so you stand out too.

When your dance is ready, perform it for your family or friends. They can give you a score out of ten. Then ask them to make up their own dance and give them a score.

This coat has a colorful lining, like "hidden feathers."

I have big boots, so I can stomp my feet in my dance.

I've got a hat and scarf as my 'special feathers'.

Amazing Bird Journeys

Many birds make long journeys every year when the seasons change. They travel because they need to find food. This is called migration and birds that do it are called migrants.

Insect Appetites

Swallows eat insects. They nest in northern parts of the world during summer, when it's warm and there are lots of insects. But the insects disappear when winter comes, so in autumn they fly south to warmer places, such as Africa and South America. Here they find plenty more insects to last the winter.

Mega Migration

The Arctic tern makes the longest bird migration. Every year, it flies from the Arctic to the Antarctic and back. One Arctic tern may travel nearly 1.24 million miles (2 million km) in its lifetime—that's like flying to the moon and back three times.

Migrants that arrive in spring are called summer visitors. They leave in autumn.

Migrants that arrive in autumn are called winter visitors. They leave in spring.

Formation Flying

Geese migrate in groups that make a V shape in the sky. This makes flying easier, because the bird in front leaves the air smoother and calmer for the ones following behind. The geese take turns to be the one in front.

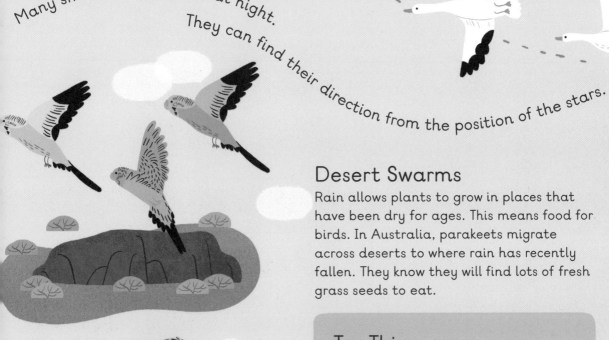

Many small birds migrate at night. They can find their direction from the position of the stars.

Desert Swarms

Rain allows plants to grow in places that have been dry for ages. This means food for birds. In Australia, parakeets migrate across deserts to where rain has recently fallen. They know they will find lots of fresh grass seeds to eat.

Try This...

Why not make your own study of migrating birds? Find out which common birds in your area are summer visitors. In spring, note the first date when you see each one. Do the same again next year to see whether the dates change. For example:

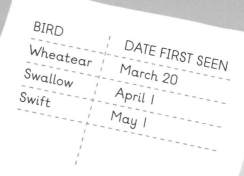

BIRD	DATE FIRST SEEN
Wheatear	March 20
Swallow	April 1
Swift	May 1

Getting Fatter

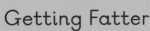

Most small birds don't feed while migrating. Instead, they eat a lot just before setting out. This extra food turns into fat, which gives them extra energy for flying. The sedge warbler eats so much before migration that it doubles its weight.

Be a Birdwatcher

The best way to learn about birds is to go out and watch them.

What Bird is it?

Here are a few ways to help identify the bird you have seen.

Size and Shape

Compare it with a bird you know. For example, is it bigger or smaller than a sparrow? Does it have any obvious features, such as a long neck or beak?

Color and Markings

What color is its plumage? Can you see any markings, such as spots or stripes?

Movement

How does it move? On the ground, does it walk or hop? In the air, does it flap fast or glide slowly?

Binoculars give you a closer view. Practice by using them on things that are close and things far away.

Be prepared to stay outside for a long time. Dress warmly and wear a raincoat if it's cold or wet, and put on sunscreen if it's hot.

Tips for better **birding**

- Keep the sun behind you, so you can see the birds' colors more clearly.
- Move slowly and quietly so as not to disturb birds. Keep your head down and your voice low.
- Go birdwatching with someone who knows about birds and can help you.

Note what you see in a **notebook** or on your phone. Take a photo or make a small drawing to look up later.

A **bird book** has pictures and descriptions to help you identify birds. Choose one that is small enough to carry and covers the birds found in your area.

Finding Birds

There are birds everywhere. You don't have to go anywhere special to see them. But the more different places you visit, the more different birds you will see.

Find out good places for birdwatching by keeping lists of all the birds you see in each place. Add new birds to each list whenever you see them. Here are some places you could try.

In the Park

All the birds you see at your local park.
- Magpie
- Heron
- Mallard

At Home

All the birds you see in your garden or around your home.
- Collared dove
- American robin
- Finch

In Town

All the birds you see when you go into town—perhaps for shopping.

- Feral pigeon
- Pied wagtail
- House sparrow

Forest, beaches, lakes, mountains, and cities are all types of **habitat**.

The place where a bird lives is called its **habitat**.

By the Seaside

All the birds you see at the beach—perhaps the birds you see on vacation.

- Oystercatcher
- Cormorant
- Herring gull

Try This

Your lists will show you which places have the most birds. Have a think about why that is. Do you see more birds where there are more trees, perhaps, or where there is some water?

Habitats and Homes

There are many different habitats around the world. Each is home to a different community of birds. All the birds that live in any particular habitat are adapted to surviving there.

The **ptarmigan** (pronounced "tarmigan") lives high in the mountains. In winter, its plumage is white so it can't be seen against the snow. In summer, when the snow disappears, its plumage changes to brown, the same color as the hillsides.

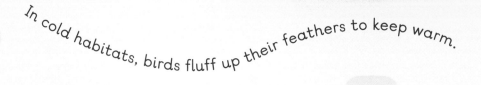

In cold habitats, birds fluff up their feathers to keep warm.

The **cactus wren** lives in deserts. It makes its home in holes inside tall cactus plants. This helps protect it from the baking desert heat. The spines on the cactus also keep away snakes that might want to eat its eggs and babies.

The **secretary bird** lives in grasslands. Long legs help it stand up tall so it can look over the long grass. Its favorite food is snakes. It uses its long legs to stamp on them without being bitten.

Many birds that live in grasslands make their nests on the grounds.

Before people built seaside towns, the **herring gull's** natural habitat was sea cliffs. Now this clever bird has learned to live in town. It nests on roofs and finds lots to eat among the waste people leave behind.

Other birds that nest in roofs include swifts, sparrows, and jackdaws.

Mini Habitats

One area can have many mini habitats. Look around your local park. There might be lawns, hedges, woodland, and perhaps a pond. Each one is a habitat that offers a home for different birds.

Noisy Birds

Birds can be very noisy—especially in spring, when most birds sing loudest. The singers are usually male. They do it to attract a female and claim a place to breed, called a **territory**. Some songs are long and beautiful. Others are short and simple.

Sky High

Skylarks sing in midair. They continue singing nonstop as they fly higher and higher. This may be exhausting, but it helps them to be heard far and wide.

Loon Lakes

Common loons give their trembling call from the middle of a lake. Each male has his own call. It says that the lake belongs to him. Other males on other lakes make slightly different calls.

Cheep Imitations

Some birds are copycats. The marsh warbler makes up his song with bits from the songs of more than 100 other types of bird. Australia's greater lyrebird can even imitate mechanical noises, such as camera shutters.

Click
Click

Headbanger

Woodpeckers can't sing. Instead males find a hollow branch and bash their beak against it very quickly. This make a very loud "rat-a-tat-tat" sound, called drumming. It works just like a song, to attract females and scare away rival males.

Click!
Click!

Can you whistle any bird songs?

Sounding the Alarm

Not all birds can sing but all birds can make calls. A call is a shorter sound used for keeping in contact or sounding the alarm. If a wren sees danger—such as a hawk or cat—it makes a rattling alarm call. This warns other wrens to watch out.

Noisy Names

The cuckoo gets its name from the noise it makes. "Cuck-koo" says the male in spring. Many other birds are named for their voices. Chiffchaff, chickadee, and hoopoe are just a few. Can you think of any others?

Catch the Dawn Chorus

You may have heard of the dawn chorus. This happens during spring, when birds all sing together early in the morning. It's the best time to enjoy birdsong—but you have to get up early.

Rise and Shine!

Choose a clear morning, without wind or rain, and head out at 6am, when the birds will be singing loudly. Go to a nearby area of greenery then find a comfy spot to sit and listen.

Tool Kit

- a notebook
- your phone
- binoculars (if possible)

Who's Singing?

Every songbird has its own voice. Concentrate on one song and try to identify the singer. Get close enough to see it—but not too close. Move slowly and be patient.

Once you've identified the bird, try to memorize its song. Listen carefully. Is the rhythm steady or jerky? Does it go up or down? How many seconds does the song last?

A singing wren sounds as though it is in a hurry to finish.

woodpigeon

Put it into Words

Some birds' songs sound like words. This makes them easier to remember. Can you hear any words when you listen to birds? Use your imagination. Write them down.

Record it

If you can't work out which bird is singing, you could film a short video of it on a phone. You can look up the picture and sound later to figure out what it might be.

Teacher, teacher!

Teacher, teacher!

Remember: Don't worry if you can't spot the birds singing. Birdsong is amazing to just listen to and enjoy.

I won't work for you!

Always tell a grown-up where you're going!

great tit

Cuckoo!

55

Be a Bird Detective

You don't have to see or hear birds to know that they're around. Birds leave other clues behind. See how many you can find.

Feathers

Look out for feathers on the ground. Compare them with pictures in a bird book to figure out which bird left the feather behind.

magpie

pheasant

blue jay

Tracking Them Down

Birds leave footprints in soft ground. Look at how big they are to figure out what kind of bird might have made them. What shape are they?

A sparrow has tiny tracks.

A goose has webbed feet.

A heron has long toes.

The pattern of a bird's tracks also shows you how the bird moves.

A pigeon takes short steps.

A thrush hops with both feet together.

Feeding

Birds also leave clues when they feed. Small holes in dead wood may show where a woodpecker pecked for grubs. A pile of feathers may be the remains of a bird killed by a hawk. Look out for nibbled fruit and other telltale signs.

Splat!

Bird droppings may be yucky to look at but they can show where birds have been. Some are distinctive: birds feeding on blackberries leave pinkish droppings; green woodpeckers leave dark, speckled droppings, full of tiny bits of ants.

Remember! Always wash your hands after touching things in nature.

Did You Know?

Owls cough up the **indigestible** bits of their food in a round pellet about the size of your thumb. It usually contains fur and tiny bones. You can find these pellets under the trees where they sleep. Look up and you might even see the owl watching you.

The King of Birds

This story is based on an old Celtic folk tale from the British Isles.

Many years ago, all the birds gathered to choose their king. They couldn't agree who it should be, so decided to settle it with a contest: whichever bird could fly the highest would win the crown.

On the big day, all the birds flew up into the air. The small birds soon grew tired—their wings weren't strong enough to fly far. Next the ducks stopped, then the crows. Soon all the birds had given up—except the eagle, who continued soaring high into the sky.

The eagle thought he'd won. But as he began gliding back down he heard a small voice calling: "I am king! I am king!" He looked up to see a tiny wren fluttering above him. She had hidden among his feathers and ridden on his back. The eagle was furious but he was too exhausted to fly any higher.

When the wren landed the small birds were delighted. They had been sure that one of the larger birds would win. But the large birds were furious. "You tricked us," they complained. "That's not fair!"

"Why is it better to be strong than to be smart?" replied the wren. "Name another challenge and I will win again." So a new contest was agreed: whichever bird could fly the lowest would be king.

Once again, all the birds took off. This time they swooped low above the ground. But the tiny wren saw a mouse hole and scurried down into it. "I am the lowest!" she called out. "I am king!"

The large birds were furious. They agreed that the wren could be king, but they were determined that she would never rule over them.

Today the wren is still the king of the birds, but she is so afraid of the angry eagles and hawks that she stays hidden in the bushes. All the other birds visit her for advice, as she is so smart.

I am king!

Templates

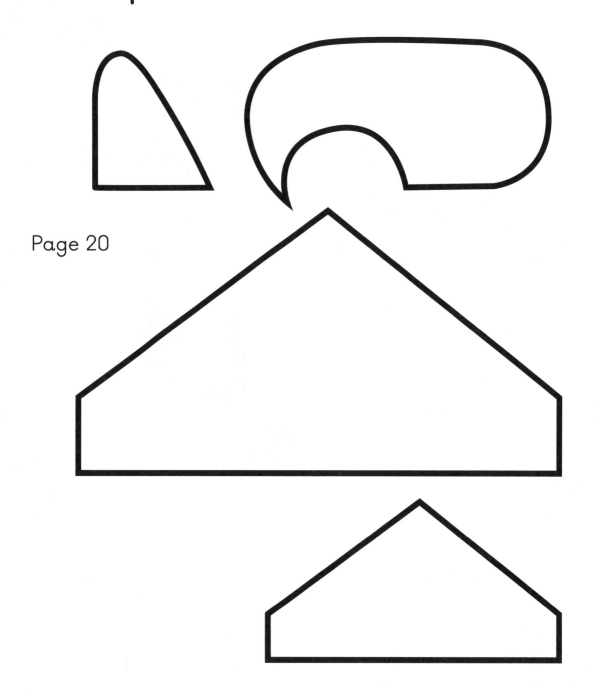

Page 20

Glossary

Adapted The way in which an animal or plant is specially shaped or equipped to survive in its environment

Air resistance The force of air pushing back if you push against it. You can feel this if you wave a piece of paper fast.

Ancestor An animal from the past that is related to one living today. For example, dinosaurs are ancestors of today's birds.

Arctic/Antarctic The Arctic is the northernmost part of the world, with the North Pole at its center. The Antarctic is the southernmost part of the world. Both are very cold and covered in snow and ice for much of the time.

Birding A popular word for birdwatching

Breeding When adults get together and produce young. Birds breed by laying eggs, which hatch into baby birds.

Camouflage Colors, shapes, or patterns on an animal that look like its background so make it hard to see. Camouflage helps animals hide from danger.

Embryo An unborn or unhatched baby animal still in the process of developing. A bird embryo develops inside an egg.

Fertilized A fertilized egg is one that is able to hatch and produce a baby.

Flippers The paddle-shaped front limbs of some swimming animals, such as seals and dolphins, that help push them through water. Some swimming birds, such as penguins, use their wings as flippers.

Habitat The type of home in which a plant or animal lives naturally. Forests, mountains, and rivers are all examples of habitats.

Incubation The period of time during which a parent bird sits on its eggs in order to keep them safe and warm while the embryo develops inside

Indigestible This describes food that is too tough or nasty-tasting for an animal to digest inside its stomach.

Ingredients Food or substances that are combined to make a larger dish. Eggs, sugar, and flour are all ingredients of a cake, for example.

Minibeasts Insects and other small creatures such as spiders, worms, and centipedes. Minibeasts are important food for many birds.

Molting The process by which a bird sheds its old, worn feathers in order to grow new, stronger ones. Most birds molt once or twice a year.

Mount Everest The highest mountain in the world. It is located in the Himalayas mountain range, between the countries of Nepal and China, and measures 29,029 feet (8,848 m) above sea level.

Plumage All the feathers on a bird's body

Rudder A flap at the back of a boat or on the tail of an aircraft that can turn left or right to help it steer. A flying bird uses its tail as a rudder by twisting it from side to side.

Species A single type of animal or plant that cannot breed with any other type. For example, a golden eagle is one of many different species of eagle.

Territory An area that a bird (or another animal) claims as its own, in which it breeds and raises its young

Thermal A spiraling current of air that rises from the ground when the ground is heated by the Sun

Vole A small, furry animal that belongs to the rodent family—like a mouse, but with smaller ears and a shorter tail

Waterhole A natural pool formed by rainwater. Waterholes in dry areas are very important places for animals to drink.

Weaving Attaching pieces of grass, sticks, or other natural material to each other by winding them together into a kind of mesh

Wingspan The distance between a bird's wing tips, when it holds its wings open

Tools of the Trade answers:
1) b, 2) d, 3) e, 4) c, 5) a

Index

Quarto is the authority on a wide range of topics.
Quarto educates, entertains and enriches the lives of our readers—enthusiasts and lovers of hands-on living.
www.quartoknows.com

MIX
Paper from responsible sources
FSC® C104723

Author: Mike Unwin
Illustrator: Pau Morgan
Consultant: Michael Bright
Editors: Carly Madden, Ellie Brough
Designers: Clare Barber, Sarah Chapman-Suire, Mike Henson

© 2019 Quarto Publishing plc

First published in 2019 by QEB Publishing, an imprint of The Quarto Group.
6 Orchard Road, Suite 100,
Lake Forest, CA 92630.
T: +1 949 380 7510
F: +1 949 380 7575
www.QuartoKnows.com

A CIP record for this book is available from the Library of Congress.

ISBN 978 1 78603 637 7
9 8 7 6 5 4 3 2 1
Manufactured in Dongguan, China TL112018